The Dance Debate

Discourses and Performance

Joseph Alagha

KNOWLEDGE WORLD
KW Publishers Pvt Ltd
New Delhi

in association with

Calcutta University
Kolkata

2011 FPBA BEST PUBLISHERS AWARD (ENGLISH)

The Court of Directors of the East India Company sent a despatch in July, 1854 to the Governor-General of India in Council, suggesting the establishment of the Universities of Calcutta, Madras and Bombay.

In pursuance of that despatch, the University of Calcutta was founded on January 24, 1857.

The University adopted in the first instance, the pattern of the University of London and gradually introduced modifications in its constitution.

ISBN 978-93-81904-12-1

KNOWLEDGE WORLD

Published in India by

Kalpana Shukla
KW Publishers Pvt Ltd
4676/21, First Floor, Ansari Road, Daryaganj, New Delhi 110002
Phone: +91 11 23263498/43528107
email: knowledgeworld@vsnl.net • www.kwpub.com

Printed and Bound in India

Contents

The Dance Debate
Discourses And Performance

"The manipulation of the body has many forms in different cultures and remains one of the most effective and most visible ways of transmitting norms and other cultural content" (Tabboni 2006: 474) .

Introduction: The debate

Few days before the beginning of Ramadan 2009, the erudite Egyptian religious scholar Gamal al-Banna – the brother of the late founder of the Muslim Brotherhood Hasan al-Banna – issued a religious edict (*fatwa*) sanctioning purposeful art, in general, and purposeful dancing, in particular. He paid tribute to the late belly dancer Tahia Carioca, whom he considered a 'committed artist'. The debate started taking root since the Egyptian weekly *Al-Wafd* published an article, 'Najwa Fouad: Prohibiting Dancing is an Encroachment on Art and Gamal Al-Banna did us [Artists] Justice'.[1] The debate reached an unprecedented height when on August 19, 2009, the daily *Al-Masry Al-Youm*[2] published al-Banna's article, 'Dancing and Islam, can they be in harmony?'[3] Every day, there appeared new critics and defenders in the readers' opinions section, which made this debate interesting to follow in the somewhat open public sphere of the Egyptian press. The main point raised in the debate seems to centre around one issue – when is a woman allowed to perform in front of an audience, and when is she banned from doing so because of the sensitivity of displaying her body in public space?

On another level, an entirely different conception of this 'purposeful dance' was propagated by a non-Islamist, the late intellectual Edward Said. He initiated the Tahia Carioca debate on October 10, 1999 in the wake of the death of the dancer. Basing his insights on a personal interview conducted ten years prior to her death as well as personal observations throughout the years, Said wrote, "Tahia Carioca was the most stunning and long-lived of the Arab world's Eastern dancers... Belly-dancing in many ways is the opposite of ballet, its Western equivalent as an art form." About her performance, Said wrote, "Eastern dancing as Tahia practiced it shows the dancer planting herself more and more solidly in the earth, digging into it almost, scarcely moving... Tahia's dancing vertically suggested a sequence of horizontal pleasures, but also paradoxically conveyed the kind of elusiveness and grace... What she did was obviously performed inside an Arab and Islamic setting... She belonged to the tradition of the *alema*, the learned woman spoken about by great observers of modern Egypt..., that is, a courtesan who was extremely literate as well as lithe and profligate with her bodily charms." Her 'untidy' and 'shiftless' life 'is true of performers in general, who really exist before us for a brief time they are on stage and then disappear', especially when thousands of her performances were not recorded; the ones that were recorded have the power and appeal to motivate the audience to 'creatively participate in the recorded artist's performance'.[4]

Edward Said wrote that she was an industrious, committed individual who cherished her Islamic sensibilities. The queen of belly dancing, a 'subversive figure' who had inspired millions, was a successful actress who also engaged in satirical theatre and political work, advocating social protest and displaying political agency, a stance that earned her a ticket to prison many times. However, in her last years as if her 'genes' rebelled against her, making her fat and no longer agile, thus hindering her from dancing, acting, or being engaged in public charitable work.[5] This was accompanied by a 'return to religion' and public piety in dress and behaviour by the late 'dancer and cultural symbol'. Edward Said added that dancing and performance are decent professions that were in line with her political activism.[6]

After this anecdote, an important clarification is required to be made at this stage. There might be a useful connection between the two debates. Tahia's dance is not 'purposeful' in any way, although she, as a person, might be. The point that I would like to make is that one has to differentiate between the person on the one hand, and the activity on the other hand. As will be highlighted later, this is a major flaw, a weakness in al-Banna's reasoning. The Lebanese case is about the activity of female dancing becoming purposeful under certain circumstances. The Egyptian debate is not about the dance per se; rather, the debate is about the dancer who might still be 'good' despite her activities.

Several scholars have addressed the sensitivity of displaying the (female) body in public, particularly in the Muslim context (Tabboni 2006; Geulen: 2006; Gole 2006; Van Nieuwkerk 2003, 1998, and 1995). This holds especially true for the moving body (Van Nieuwkerk 2011). The sensitivity is reflected in religious discourses by both the Sunni and Shi'ite religious scholars. Dancing and public bodily performances by both sexes are not only addressed by al-Banna, who seems to mix the person with the activity (agency), but also by Ayatullah Fadlallah and Hizbullah. Ayatullah Fadlallah is renowned for his progressive views on women and his defence of women's rights, including their right to contest the public space, which is usually dominated by men, especially in Muslim majority societies. It is interesting to compare al-Banna's views on the body and public space, as a Sunni progressive religious scholar, on the one hand, with those of Ayatullah Fadlallah, as a Shi'ite progressive religious authority, and Hizbullah as a progressive Islamic movement that puts Ayatullah Fadlallah's views into practice, on the other hand. Hizbullah empowered its veiled women to contest the public space, including mixing with men and performing on stage for the aim of purposeful art, or 'resistance art', as Hizbullah calls it. Hizbullah defines 'resistance art' as a specific genre of purposeful art that deals with political and social themes such as jihad, sacrifice, and patriotism.

Another clarification is required to be addressed at this stage. Regarding the concept of *maslaha* (interest), I would like to situate myself within existing literature in order to show how my empirical Islamic studies' approach differs from existing scholarship. This warrants a short discussion on the notion of *maslaha*. From a social science perspective, Craig Calhoun cautions, "For interests [*masalih*, pl. of *maslaha*] to be anything other than completely ephemeral preferences, they must be analysable in terms of the identities of social actors" (2003: 255). According to Salvatore and Levine, "*Maslaha* is the 'cause or source of something good or beneficial', which conveys the full scale of positive values from 'uncorrupted' up to 'right', 'honest', 'virtuous', and 'just'" (Shami 2009: 70). They add, in practice, socio-religious or Islamic movements employ the concept of *maslaha* in order 'to achieve political, social, and cultural justice' (p. 81). Instead of entirely relying on the social science perspective employed above, I add the Islamic studies' approach in which I ground the study of the concept in a specific context. In other words, the difference in my approach and fieldwork material is the empirical Islamic studies' contextual approach that I am going to apply to performing arts. I employ *maslaha* as a teleological interpretation in relation to art with a purpose (*al-fann al-hadif*), evaluating how religious scholars employ this concept to legitimatise purposeful dancing.

What are the differences and commonalities between progressive Sunni and Shi'ite views on purposeful art, in general, and purposeful dancing, in particular? What is the view of the Egyptian 'liberal reformer' religious scholar Gamal al-Banna? What is Hizbullah's view on 'resistance art', and how does it comport with Ayatullah Fadlallah's views on the body and dancing in public space? This article relies on extensive interview material with Hizbullah's rank and file, fieldwork observations, as well as primary Arabic and secondary English sources.

The article is divided into three main parts – first, I will describe the discourse on art, in particular, performing art, for male and female performers. I will start with al-Banna and then compare his views to those of Fadlallah; second, I will analyse the underlying logic of interest (*maslaha*) and the ways of reasoning employed by al-Banna and Fadlallah to legitimise bodily performances in public space. I will highlight similarities and differences between the two, and third, I will deal with Hizbullah's ideas and practice on dancing, and the permissibility of female performances in public space, highlighting how they consciously put Fadlallah's discourses in practice. This results in a cultural practice that is remarkably similar to al-Banna. Thus, al-Banna is indirectly influential on Hizbullah, or Hizbullah is indirectly influenced by al-Banna. In conclusion, I will analyse the similarities and differences among the three: al-Banna, Fadlallah, and Hizbullah.

Discourses on Art, Performing Art, and Dancing

In this section, I compare the discourse on art and dancing of al-Banna with Fadlallah's ruling. As mentioned above, al-Banna is an erudite Egyptian religious scholar and the brother of the late founder of the Muslim Brotherhood, Hasan al-Banna. The late Ayatullah Sayyid Muhammad Husayn Fadlallah (1935-2010) was the highest-ranking Shi'ite religious authority (*marja'*) in Lebanon and one of Hizbullah's early ideologues.

Al-Banna[7]

Al-Banna answered the question 'Is dancing compatible with Islam?' in the affirmative, heavily quoting the Islamic primary and secondary sources in a systematic, didactic manner. He argued that Islam is a social practice and that Islamic law (*Shari'ah*) is a socially constructed phenomenon.[8] On these grounds, al-Banna rendered an authoritative ruling, based on Islamic law, sanctioning purposeful dancing.

The debate raged when Al-Banna argued that purposeful dancing is a 'noble, decent profession', and the late belly dancer Tahia Carioca was 'a committed artist with a respectable history'. He clarified that the prohibitions against art were not directed against art per se, but rather against everything that is 'beautiful' such as literature, poetry, music, singing, and women. Al-Banna stressed that these prohibitions reflect only the individual whim of the prohibitors who regard many positive things in a negative light. He downgrades 'modernist' and 'liberal' readings of Islam, and even classifies them as 'infidel' and 'heretic'. Al-Banna argues that this fundamentalist reading or interpretation of Islam renders the religious doctrine 'barren, dry, and uncreative', since the Qur'an sanctions freedom of thought and religion.[9] When one of al-Banna's admirers told him to issue a denial against what has been attributed to him, that is, purposeful dancing is a 'noble, decent profession', al-Banna said, "Why should I? Dancing is the most eloquent, creative manifestation of bodily performance." His answer split commentators into three groups: accusers, centralists (holders of reconciliatory discourse), and defenders.[10]

Al-Banna's accusers charged him with inferiority complex and identity crisis, whereby he is willing to do anything to reach the same status as his late brother. Some of the critics targeted al-Banna on a personal level, wondering how he would feel if his daughter was to strip-dance in a nightclub. A minority labelled him as 'an enemy of Islam whose mission is to rupture the moral fibre of Muslim society'. Others doubted his religious credentials arguing that he is not entitled to issue *fatwas*. The late reformist thinker Hamid Nasr Abu Zayd (1943-2010) – who in 1995 was banished from Egypt to the Netherlands for his unorthodox reading of the Qur'an[11] – weighed in on the debate questioning al-Banna's credentials, "He is not a mufti; he is not a specialist, and does not have the required rigorous training in *fatwa* giving and in exercising independent reasoning (*ijtihad*)."[12]

The centralists – those advocating a reconciliatory stance – supported al-Banna's argument, namely, that God would not necessarily inflict his rage on female dancers per se, without due consideration to the content and context of their acts. On the contrary, if the dancer is engaged in virtuous, charitable acts that override and erase bad acts, God will grant her salvation and open heaven's doors to her: "Do not condemn, or else you will be condemned. God knows best."

Gamal al-Banna's defenders argued that those who condemned him misunderstood his message since he did not sanction any dance in the absolute. Rather, al-Banna severely blasted indecent dirty dancing that falls in the category of debaucheries (*al-fawahish*)[13], or types of dancing that lead to negative diversion (*lahu*) from purposeful activities, or those kinds of dancing that encourage the pursuit of pastime per se. In other words, al-Banna does not legitimise dancing as such; rather, he has argued that dancing could be a decent profession if practiced within the domain of purposeful art. Al-Banna defines purposeful art as ideologically motivated art, which aims at rectifying individuals and reforming society by portraying art as pious-moral productions in line with Islamic values, norms, and religious sensibilities.[14] The section below discusses Fadlallah's general practice and views, his restrictions and prohibitions, and under which conditions he sanctioned dancing.

Fadlallah

Was Ayatullah Fadlallah as 'liberal' as al-Banna in his views pertaining to dancing? Fadlallah defined dancing as such: "By dancing is intended this well-known art that expresses by way of bodily movements (performance) certain ideas."[15] He affirmed, "I do not consider the profession of dancing and singing, which preserves moral obligations, to be prohibited... Needless to say in this sense that although we allow certain things for the lack of evidence that prohibits them, we at the same time take into consideration the social restrictions."[16] Ayatullah Fadlallah legitimised women's participation in the field of theatre and movie, including dancing and public performance: "We do not see any illegitimacy as long as this job does not contradict with our Islamic path. Furthermore, I do not only encourage such activities, but I see them as a must since they help in enlightening our people on all levels politically, socially and morally as well. Therefore, I encourage Muslim women to take part in public performance due to its greatest advantages to the Islamic cultural sphere, and at the same time due to the greatest role Muslim women could be performing."[17]

According to Ayatullah Fadlallah, dancing takes many shapes: those that are acceptable, and those that are lowbrow and lead to vice. By definition, prohibited dancing is the 'sleazy', 'morally depraved one'; it is this dancing that expresses 'infatuation, sexual desire, and lust'. In this context, gender does not matter: there is no difference between the dancer being a woman or a man; no difference if she/he is wearing decent clothes or showing parts of the body that should be covered. In addition, there is no difference if the audience are gender segregated or mixed. In all of these instances, dancing is prohibited. Based on the aforementioned, it is not sanctioned for a woman to dance in a wedding in front of a female audience if her dancing is 'sleazy' and full of 'debaucheries'.[18]

Ayatullah Fadlallah stressed that sanctioned dancing is diametrically opposed to the above. For instance, it is the one that is purposeful: it expresses positive vigilance (*hamas*) (cf. Fayyad's argument below) and chivalry, or emulates movements in nature such as that of the birds and the wind, or it expresses historical events and the likes, including folkloric dances (such a *dabke*), which are performed in joyful occasions. These artistic expressions are sanctioned on condition that they are not accompanied by indulgence in vices that are against the norms of decency, and any behaviour that is prohibited in its own right (in the absolute), or a behaviour that becomes prohibited due to secondary edicts.[19] He explained that if a woman moved her body in a normal, acceptable way, then it is not *haraam* (religiously prohibited).[20]

Ayatullah Fadlallah stated that his followers are not allowed to watch any kind of dancing if they suspect that it would lead to their 'moral degeneration' or 'corrupt' their character. It is also prohibited to employ others to engage in the above and make money or make a living out of such 'debaucheries'.[21] He explained that as a matter of principle, young girls, below the age of religious obligation (girls in their early teens), are allowed to dance without a veil in front of men. However, precautions need to be taken to prevent such happy occasions of entertainment from degenerating into indecency. In this case, dancing becomes forbidden due to secondary considerations, rather than primary or absolute prohibitions.[22] Fadlallah added that seductive or 'expressive bodily dancing' in front of a mixed audience is prohibited for both males and females, since in the public domain, excessive bodily movement is not allowed. He argued that moderation is the norm since 'Islam is the religion of the golden mean' (*al-Islam din al-wasat*).

In an interview, Ayatullah Fadlallah clarified to me that when a woman performs in public space, she goes out as a human being, not as a female body that demeans her status: "She goes out as reason, will, movement, and a beautiful image conducive to the promotion of 'resistance art' or 'purposeful art'."[23] He told me that the issue is not putting a veil on her head even if it is a religious obligation; rather, the performer should place a veil on her heart, instincts, and temptations. He reiterated that the main issue is to be a human being first and foremost, irrespective of gender. According to Fadlallah, a woman can practice any profession and interact in public space, as long as she abides by the ethical values, norms, and religious sensibilities of Islam.[24]

From the aforementioned, it is interesting to note that al-Banna and Fadlallah are delivering the same message or saying the same thing, but they have used a different packaging that caters to the needs of their constituencies. Both of them agree that Islam is the religion of moderation capable of addressing apparent problems that address man's livelihood in a changing, dynamic world. Both concur that the corpus of Islamic traditions sanctions purposeful dancing, which by definition is free from debaucheries, and thus, caters to Muslim sensibilities. I will now compare the underlying ways of reasoning on which Ayatullah Fadlallah and Gamal al-Banna base their discourses.

Ways of reasoning: *maslaha* and *hasanat*

Even though the notion of *maslaha* (interest) has a negative connotation in Middle Eastern societies on a popular level, the same notion has gained a positive reception in Muslim jurisprudence. Although the Islamic jurisprudential concept of *maslaha* is a secondary source of Islamic law, in Shi'ite jurisprudence, it can take precedence over primary sources of law, even the five pillars, if the context and circumstance require recourse to such an action. For instance, Imam Khumayni's 1988 fatwa stipulated that the *maslaha* of the Islamic order, or its agencies, gains priority over any other principle in social and political affairs, including prayer, pilgrimage, and fasting (Alagha 2006: 88-92, 164-165). How do religious scholars such as al-Banna and Fadlallah employ the *maslaha* argument?

Al-Banna[25]

In order to render an authoritative opinion based on the Islamic law sanctioning purposeful dancing, al-Banna dwelled on two theories: (1) the Islamic theory of human nature and values, and (2) the Islamic conception of justice. The common ground between them is purposefulness in relation to the jurisprudential concept of *hasanat* (good deeds) or interest *maslaha*. First, I will examine the Islamic theory of human nature and values.

According to al-Banna, God created man from clay and blew His spirit into him, giving him conscience and will; and at the same time, God implanted the sexual instinct, one of the strongest instincts, moulding in him both piety and malice, thus distancing him from the world of angels who are impeccable and infallible. Al-Banna adds that God left man an easy pray to the devils who seduce him with all temptations, the most prominent being 'power, women, and wealth'. In spite of this reasoning, al-Banna considers human beauty, as it is personified in a woman -- the most perfect beauty.

Then God sent his messengers and divine books to guide man to salvation, but He gave him freedom of will to choose belief or unbelief, guidance or waywardness. God left man to choose the path he pleases, and at the same time, God provided everything he needs so that he will never be in need [Qur'an: (91: 7-10) and (92: 5)].

Al-Banna clarifies that this discussion on the guilt of human weakness is different from the guilt emanating from evil deeds such as theft, rape, murder, etc.; deeds that are punishable and deterred by law. Al-Banna adds that man is bound to err because of his nature; this fact is borne out by social practice. Consequently, erring is part of reality and a manner of surrendering to human nature and subordination to social nature (action and reaction). Al-Banna contends that the characteristic in man to sin is a part of his original nature. That is why Islam opened the doors for repentance and asking for forgiveness. What is better than both is to do good: Qur'an (11: 114): "For those things that are good remove those that are evil."[26]

This is the first cornerstone and the jurisprudential rule that al-Banna bases his argument for sanctioning purposeful dancing upon. He clarifies that if a woman was dancing day and night, but at the same time, she was engaged in good works and deeds, caring for others, reforming the self, etc., then her good deeds (*hasanat, masalih*) would not only outweigh but also conquer her bad deeds (*sayyi'at, mafasid*). According to him, this is due to the merciful-divinely providence, which stresses and judges according to the intention and purpose.[27] A thorough reading might reveal that this conclusion does not logically follow from the above, and it seems closer to the second theory. Possibly al-Banna is suggesting an organic link between the two.

The second theory that al-Banna uses to sanction purposeful dancing is the Islamic conception of justice. According to al-Banna, the Islamic conception of justice has to do with the judgment on man. Justice on earth is based upon chastising the wrongdoers, but not rewarding the good doers. This is mainly due to the scarcity of resources. However, God's resources in paradise are always in abundance; that is why it adds to the punishment of the wrongdoers the reward of the good doers.

Al-Banna contends that what distinguishes divine justice is not that it condemns sinners to fire (hell), since this could happen here and now where sinners are punished in the courts of law. Rather, the distinguishing trait of divine justice is that it rewards the righteous, the philanthropists. So millions, even billions, enter heaven. Those who have spent their life toiling without any enjoyment or leisure will abundantly enjoy the fruits of heaven. As mentioned in the Qur'an (47: 15): "...rivers of wine, a joy to those who drink; and rivers of honey pure and clear..."

He adds that a common but wrong misconception is that when man sins, he is severely punished and may end up being in hell. In addition, he will be asked whether he regularly performed the duty of prayer. If he were found negligent, then nothing would help him since hell fire would have devoured him.

Al-Banna affirms, "Verily, punishment is not inflicted unless the concept of *maslaha* is upheld, whereby a meticulous balancing act is performed between good deeds and bad deeds to see which one outweighs the other," which is close to previous conclusion. He quotes the Qur'an: (101: 6-9) "Then, he whose balance (of good deeds) will be (found) heavy, he will be in a life of good pleasure and satisfaction. But he whose balance (of good deeds) will be (found) light, — he will have his home in a (bottomless) Pit."

Al-Banna adds that the weight of the good deeds and bad deeds might be different than what we expect. A good deed might be multiplied 700 times as the Qur'an (2: 261) conveys: "The parable of those who spend their substance in the way of Allah is that of a grain of corn: it groweth seven ears, and each ear Hath a hundred grains. Allah giveth manifold increase to whom He pleaseth: And Allah careth for all and He knoweth all things." However, a bad deed is simply bad; it could be big or it could be small, but it cannot be doubled or have its weight proportional to its bulk.

There are also bad deeds, which God waivers and removes from the scale due to His mercy and kindness, as stated in the Qur'an (46: 16): "Such are they from whom We shall accept the best of their deeds and pass by their ill deeds: (They shall be) among the Companions of the Garden: a promise! of truth, which was made to them (in this life)." This is because the mercy of man amounts to one per cent of the mercy of God; this mercy might encompass anything. Al-Banna concludes by reiterating the fulcrum of his argument – 'without rewarding the righteous, justice cannot be consummated'.

This theory of justice is the second cornerstone and the most salient jurisprudential rule that al-Banna bases his argument upon to legitimise purposeful dancing. He argues that there are despicable deeds, by far worse than dancing, even if that dancing were performed naked. He explains what he meant by posing the following rhetorical question: How does the dancing of a woman, on the one hand, comport with unjust state laws; inhumane torturing in prisons; defilement of human worth and dignities; and even unjustified one-sided *fatwas*, which cause so much misery and hardships to the people, fatwas that are issued by those who claim to 'enjoin the good and prohibit the evil'[28], but fall into vices and malevolence instead, on the other hand? He stresses that it is not farfetched for a dancer to be in the heaven of heavens, for the mercy of God is much, much more than we can ever conceive. According to al-Banna, if most people think otherwise, it is precisely because our earthly justice condemns the guilty persons for their bad deeds, but does not reward them for their good deeds and philanthropy, and this is 'deficient justice by all means'. Al-Banna concludes that it is possible for dancing to be in harmony with Islamic teachings if it is purposeful.

There appears to be an inconsistency in al-Banna's views since he concludes that if the person can have a positive balance between *masalih* and *mafasid*, then this makes the bad act itself in harmony with Islam, which does not make much sense. As I pointed out in the beginning of the article, al-Banna seems to be swapping the person with the acts. This is something not done in the Lebanese Shi'ite view, since they are discussing the activity itself and the balance between the *masalih* and *mafasid* of the activity in question, not the person. This substantial difference cannot be overlooked when comparing al-Banna's views with Fadlallah's and Hizbullah's views.

Fadlallah

Concerning the sensitivity of the body and performance in public space, Ayatullah Fadlallah laid down the general jurisprudential rule according to which choices would be made concerning prohibition or sanctioning: 'everything that has negative effects and whose disadvantages [*mafasid*] is more than its advantages [*masalih*] is considered prohibited'.[29]

Ayatullah Fadlallah was referring to an important secondary source in Islamic Law, which Muslim religious scholars employ to determine if a certain practice – such as dancing and public performance – is permitted, neutral, or forbidden. In particular, Ayatullah Fadlallah was making reference to one of the maxims of Islamic jurisprudence: 'the warding off of vices is preferable to obtaining interests' or 'the avoidance of vice is always preferable to any benefit that might accrue from the act'. This calls for an explanation. Ayatullah Fadlallah clarifies that when a person is confronted with two injunctions that require the exercise of his reason, reason (the mind) tells him that God has imposed on human beings injunctions for the sake of the *masalih* (advantages/virtues) and *mafasid* (disadvantages/vices, evils). In this case, what takes precedence is either the warding off of the grave disadvantage or the following of the most salient advantage. Thus, the injunction is carried out on the basis of waiving the less important injunction in favour of the more salient one. Ayatullah Fadlallah goes on to the extent of affirming that a religious injunction could be frozen under pressuring social circumstances, which relegate this injunction to a category of lower importance, so that it can be overridden by an injunction that has high priority or importance, that is, takes precedence over it. Thus, the injunction remains into effect and binding, but it can be annulled under some circumstances, if necessity (*maslaha*) deems it to be so (Fadlallah 2009: 82-83).[30]

Ayatullah Fadlallah, who is known for his progressive views, issued an edict sanctioning the restitution of virginity if certain conditions were met.[31] In line with his view in support of the contextual argument (i.e. no prohibition in the absolute, rather the context dictates prohibition or sanctioning), Fadlallah stressed that a woman has an inalienable right to her own body and that she can use it in a purposeful (*hadif*) way. Nevertheless, he clarified the purpose of dancing or public performance makes it *halal* or *haraam*. It is absolutely *haraam* if it is intended to arouse sexual desires and indulgence in vices, since 'everything that is based on falsehood (*batil*) is itself falsehood'. Beside that, everything else is sanctioned.[32]

If we compare the ways of reasoning of al-Banna and Fadlallah, we see that Gamal al-Banna came up with an innovative interpretation. Basing himself on classical Sunni conceptions of Islamic law – such as analogical reasoning (*qiyas*) – he employed an interpretation that looks very similar to Shi'ite interpretations, while, at the time, upholding the Sunni line of reasoning. Nevertheless, he broadened the mandate of independent reasoning (*ijtihad*) and opened its doors wide open, after allegedly being closed for centuries. Building on the unifying[33] Islamic jurisprudential conception of advantages-disadvantages (*maslaha-mafsadah*) – from the stance of his earlier argument on 'the Islamic theory of human nature and values' and 'the Islamic conception of justice' – al-Banna concluded that the justice of Islam 'balances' between good deeds and bad ones according to the measures of divine justice and mercy: 'this is the Islam that we preach and live by'.[34]

Interestingly, Fadlallah's eloquence and foresight resulted in a qualification of his argument, thus leaving the matter open to various interpretations: "Meanwhile, I think that when Muslims' conditions change and many unfamiliar habits become familiar, such issues, especially if people distinguish between legal art and the illegal one, might become familiar to them. That is why we find ourselves so far cautious about these professions [singing and dancing] trying to figure out what benefits [*maslaha*] Islam." This is telling; in line with his and al-Banna's belief that Islam is a social practice and that Islamic law is a socially constructed phenomenon, it seemed Fadlallah implied that a ruling, or a religious edict, could be revised, even abrogated (overridden) in light of a change in religious sensibilities and societal norms. This pragmatic, progressive thinking is in conformity with the nature of Shi'ite jurisprudence as well as al-Banna's interpretation of *hasanat* (good deeds) – *sayyi'at* (bad deeds) in the Sunni tradition.

This precept of practice is also warranted in social science. The above ties in nicely with Giddens' conclusion, "The reflexivity of modern social life consists in the fact that social practices are constantly examined and refined in the light of incoming information about these very practices, thus constructively altering their character" (Giddens 1990). Thus, in knowledge production and dissemination, one has to keep in mind that Islam is a social practice that is constantly undergoing revision.

Now we move from Ayatullah Fadlallah, one of Hizbullah's main ideologies, in order to see how the party's leading cadres explain their discourse on art, which serves as an embodiment of and a practical application of Fadlallah's views, and interestingly of al-Banna's insights too, at least indirectly.

Hizbullah's ideas and practice

The Lebanese resistance movement Hizbullah is not monolithic. In conformity with its policy to change as circumstances themselves change, the party's internal structure allows it to operate on a number of levels. Hizbullah is a sophisticated, complex, multifaceted, multilayered organisation, composed of at least four main divisions: (1) the 'military wing': the *jihadi* and 'terrorist' branch, (2) the social services, NGOs, and civil institutions branch, (3) the 'political wing' branch, and (4) the cultural politics branch or 'resistance art'. The rapid evolution of Hizbullah from a marginal splinter group to a dominant group in national and international politics did not come at the expense of its endorsement of cultural and artistic productions; rather, it gave it more weight and visibility in public space (Alagha 2009 and 2011). Hizbullah embarked on altering the plight of the Lebanese Shi'ites from being marginalised and oppressed to being empowered, not only in politics but also in culture and public spaces. In addition to its integration in the Lebanese public sphere, when the party rose to fame, Hizbullah resorted to the common language of art in order to convey its cultural face through art with a purpose.

Because of the importance of cultural politics to Hizbullah, the Party has founded three institutional centres that deal with cultural productions and performance. These are headed by three leading shaykhs: Shaykh Akram Barakat, the head of the *Cultural Islamic Al-Ma'arif Association*; Shaykh 'Ali Daher, the head of Hizbullah's Cultural Unit; and Shaykh Shafiq Jaradi, the Rector of *Al-Ma'arif Al-Hikmiyya College*. I have interviewed all of them in order to stress the originality of my work and the empirical, contextual Islamic studies approach I am applying.

We can clearly see the influence of Fadlallah's way of reasoning on the cadres of Hizbullah. In an interview, Hizbullah's Shaykh Akram Barakat conveyed to me the same line of thinking. He clarified that Shi'ite traditions, enjoin the pursuit of 'purposeful fun' and leisure activities within the domain of certain religious safeguards. According to him, art, performance, and dancing are not in themselves *haraam*; further, things that were previously *haraam* could become *halal* and vice versa. In other words, prohibition or sanctioning has to do with the variables of time, place, and environment; what have to be kept in mind are the aim, goal, and purpose. Islam calls for progress in all domains: reform in art elevates human worth and values. As such, the basis of Shi'ite jurisprudence is the call for innovation and modernity in order to be up-to-date with all aspects of life. God does not judge solely on the basis of the results, rather the intentions. This notion leaves room for jurisprudential innovations.

Along similar lines, Shaykh Barakat clarifies that Islam is social practice; by analogy, an artistic expression is a humanistic endeavour, not a religious one. As such, the cultural productions of Muslims reflect the environment in which they live in. Islam has no problem whatsoever with diversity; on the contrary, Islam believes that diversity enriches culture. According to Barakat, Islam stresses general safeguards that have to do with the nature of man. Hizbullah's cultural productions are oriented towards the realisation of these goals.[35] It seems Fadlallah's and Barakat's reasoning bears a striking resemblance to Gamal al-Banna's progressive thinking.

As already mentioned in the introduction and is going to be discussed in detail in the next section, Hizbullah relates interest (*maslaha*) to reform, resistance, mobilisation, and political struggle; for that reason, the party regards art as 'resistance art'. I will discuss Hizbullah's view on art, resistance art, gender mixing, and the role '*maslaha*' plays in their legitimisation of these issues.

Art

Hizbullah's deputy Secretary General, Shaykh Na'im Qasim argues that art is sanctioned in its capacity as a purposeful mobilisational tool.[36] Hajj Ghalib Abu Zaynab, Hizbullah's officer for Muslim-Christian dialogue, defines art as social art that deals with people's humanistic and social causes, aimed at 'polishing and sharpening potential skills'. From this perspective, it is labelled as positive art. 'Resistance is a positive act: resisting oppression and crying for freedom are legitimate in order to rectify the present imbalance, but with temperance as Prophet Muhammad has enjoined: "You are the *umma* of moderation (*wasatiyya*)". Thus, moderation in life is the standard norm and value that we ought to follow, as it is the precept of practice of the Prophetic Tradition. Abu Zaynab regards resistance as a social reflection to the ills rupturing the moral fibre of the community.

Resistance art

Shaykh 'Ali Daher refers to this trend of art as resistance art. He explains that though it branches from purposeful Islamic art, it is distinguished by its content and message, which deal with political and social issues as well as themes such as jihad, sacrifice, patriotism, and the like, in relation to the theory of human nature. Daher is against purposeless art or 'art for the sake of art'; rather, he is for purposeful art. In other words, Daher regards resistance art as a specific genre of purposeful art, which is distinguished by its subject matter.[37]

According to Abu Zaynab, resistance art promotes ethical and spiritual beauty and stresses the concept of God's mercy. Abu Zaynab clarifies that resistance art aims at 'promoting justice, meritocracy, integrity, and philanthropy'. He stresses that resistance art is not alien to society; rather, it is part and parcel of it. It expresses the will of society and addresses people's sensibilities and emotions. He adds, 'resistance art is an embodiment of greater jihad, societal jihad, the jihad against the self and its corrupt desires'. Abu Zaynab adds that resistance art contributes to the development of society in a positive way, thus 'guiding society away from darkness (evil) into light (virtues) by reforming the self and morals'. According to him, the evidence that resistance art is of a refined calibre is its employment in Hizbullah's media institutions and the Islamic Republic of Iran's cultural activities.[38]

According to Muhammad Kawtharani, the second man in command of Hizbullah's Cultural Unit, the role of resistance art lies in the conversion of the elements of power and realising them in Hizbullah's 'resistance society'. He defines resistance art as the art of Islamic revival or renaissance (*nuhud*) that revitalises the *umma* and wakes it up from its hibernation; the art that moves emotions and feelings to struggle against invasion, occupation, and oppression. In line with Hizbullah's resource mobilisation, this cultural resistance puts the Party's artistic capabilities to the test through promoting resistance art and gender mixed performances on stage for a mixed audience.[39]

More importantly, the three heads of Hizbullah's cultural politics institutions assured me that resistance art is conducive to the development of a 'full, coalescent human being' (*al-insan al-kamil al-mutakamil*). From this perspective, leisure activities that promote 'pious entertainment' or 'fun' are important for perpetuating a self-confident, industrious, and productive human being.[40]

Gender mixing

For Hizbullah to approve gender mixing, public performance, and acting and dancing on stage during the noble, sombre occasion of the birth of Imam al-Mahdi, a heated debate among the three heads of Hizbullah's cultural politics institutions ensued, to see whether to legitimise this social practice and what are the religious prohibitions, safeguards that ought to be taken into account. Hizbullah's Deputy Security General Shaykh Na'im Qasim along with Shaykh Muhammad Yazbik, head of the Religio-Judicial Council, were asked to adjudicate, and they ruled in favour.[41] Thus, Hizbullah was able to cater to the religious sensibilities of its constituency, in spite of all the religious prohibitions which usually bar many Islamic movements from engaging in such cultural activities, which renders Hizbullah as a 'counter-public' to them, as will be argued later.

Similar to Ayatullah Fadlallah, Shaykh Shafiq Jaradi told me that Shi'ite intellectual jurisprudential thought sanctions the mixing of genders in artistic works and performance as long as Islamic values, norms, and mores are respected. Since the artists aspire to the same goals and aims of purposeful art, then there is no prohibition in dancing together or acting together.[42]

Likewise, Hajj Muhammad Ra'd – the current head of Hizbullah's parliamentary bloc and *Shura* (Consultative) Council member – argues that Hizbullah's guidelines of behaviour and performance are dynamic, and open to developments and changing social practices. The rule of thumb is to uphold jurisprudential foundations, while taking into consideration the universal human values and ethical standards that are in concordance with religious values. If these stipulations are observed, then gender mixing is sanctioned. From this perspective, Hizbullah engages in art and creativity without encroaching upon its jurisprudential foundations and religious safeguards. In conformity with al-Banna's theory, Ra'd affirms that the religious safeguards, which aim to portray the image of the human being in society, are based upon human values rather than bodily and sexual temptations. According to Ra'd, the main aim of purposeful art is to elevate the soul so as not to slip into the dungeons of temptations and material desires.[43] In a similar vein, the head of Hizbullah's educational unit, professor of sociology at the Lebanese University and ex-director of the Party's think tank, MP Ali Fayyad clarifies that Hizbullah sanctions 'fun' or pious entertainment, but not seduction (*ighwa'*) and debaucheries. He adds that any artistic expression or performance that leads to negative relaxation or idleness (*istirkha'*) is condemned; while the one that leads to positive vigilance (*hamas*) is praised.[44]

Thus, Hizbullah sanctions mixing of the sexes in artistic productions within the domain of the religious prohibitions and religious safeguards that cater to the religious sensibilities of the audience.

The role of maslaha

Hizbullah's cultural politics is circumstantial and contextual, based upon and legitimised by the Shi'ite jurisprudential concept of interest (*maslaha*). Hajj Muhammad Ra'd argues that there is no conflict between Hizbullah's Islamic identity and its cultural productions since there is no big practical difference between the two. Ra'd adds that Hizbullah bases itself on the following rule of thumb: what falls within the domain of the legally prohibited (*haraam shar'i*), Hizbullah endeavours to prevent from coming into being or Hizbullah stands in its way; what stands in sharp contrast to the legally sanctioned (*halal shar'i*), Hizbullah tries to abort it or append it; what falls within the domain of the 'permitted' (*mubah*), Hizbullah does its best to find the most just implementation in conformity with its religious vision. Thus, according to Ra'd, Hizbullah's cultural politics is based on two basic principles: (1) keeping away the vices (*al-mafasid*) has precedent over advancing interests (*al-masalih*), and (2) the confrontation between the most damaging and the least damaging. In conformity with *ijtihad* (independent reasoning), Ra'd concludes that the jurisprudential principles, which constitute the bases for artistic expressions, sanction a great margin of manoeuvre and leeway in performance in public space.[45]

Hizbullah's 'Publics'

While al-Banna's and Fadlallah's argument is grounded in, and remains confined to, the Islamic cultural sphere, Hizbullah broadens their mandate by propagating an argument that transcends the Islamic cultural sphere into practice. It portrays the party's resistance art as both a 'resistance public' and 'a counter-public'. A resistance public to the hegemony of the state and its institutions; a counter-public to other Islamic movements who confine women to the private sphere of the family out of fear of encroaching on the religious safeguards, prohibitions, and sensitivities that govern an Islamist society. In this regard, Hizbullah portrays its post-Islamist face (Alagha 2011). While Islamists are concerned with religiosity and strict adherence to the laws, Hizbullah as a post-Islamist movement, observes these, but transcends them by pursuing a policy opening-up (*infitah*) to global cultural trends while preserving indigenous values as an Islamic moral alternative. In this regard, it is interesting to note that Fraser (1992: 122-123) and Warner (2002: 114-124) argue that publics as spaces of contestation 'are (continually) *emergent* rather than stable units. Publics and counter-publics form through, and in relation to, certain discourses, texts, performances, structures and institutions' (Shami 2009: 33). Most likely, this characterisation also applies to Hizbullah. As I will argue, by a special mould of agency and empowerment interpreted along Islamic lines, Hizbullah emerges not only as a resistance public to the state and its institutions, but also as a counter-public to other Islamic movements, precisely because of its progressive stance on the female body and performance in public space.

Göle argues, "Through the body, different personal stories and histories of diverse cultural groups become visible, hence distinguishable under the public gaze. As physical and cultural realities, bodies resist and subvert the silencing of difference of languages, opinions and ideas [i.e. act as both resistance and counter-publics]. Public spaces become performative spaces in which asymmetrical power relations between secular [state] and religious actors [Hizbullah] and imaginaries are displayed" (2006: 39).

In light of the above quote, Hizbullah could be viewed as a 'resistance public'-- as a counter cultural identity against the hegemony of the state and lack of its legitimacy. Their dancing, or performance in public space, became a space for challenging and resisting certain dominant ideologies or holders of power. As 'resistance publics', their artistic expressions, especially dancing become a public space for contesting, challenging, and resisting certain dominant ideologies or holders of power.

Also, one could argue that Hizbullah is not only a resistance public (Alagha 2011) to the state, but also a counter-public to other Islamic movements who reject the distraction of music, theatre, and performance and aim at eradicating 'places of pleasure and leisure' such as 'cafes, video and dance clubs, cinemas and certain sports clubs' (Roy 1994: 80-81). Although both Hizbullah and other Islamic movements portray sensitivity towards what they consider as 'the corrupting influence of Western Culture', Hizbullah does not hesitate to engage in (1) gender mixing in acting and revolutionary theatre on stage, and (2) in forming a one hundred-man orchestra that plays more than forty musical instruments, most of which are Western. Thus, Hizbullah succeeded in creating 'Islamised spaces' or 'alternative' spaces in order to practice and promote 'pious entertainment' and leisure activities (Alagha 2011). And so, Hizbullah's performance is viewed as a counter cultural identity against the hegemony and lack of legitimacy of the state and its institutions on the one hand, and as a reaction against other Islamic movements' reading of the 'return to Islam', which bars performance altogether as 'un-Islamic', on the other hand.

Unlike Islamic movements, which treat women as 'private property', as a counter-public to these Islamic movements, Hizbullah accords women a prominent role in the public sphere and regards them as valuable assets who are becoming more and more visible in contesting the public space with other actors, and even dominating it in some instances. Thus, Hizbullah is a counter-public to other Islamic movements who consider acting and dancing on stage as well as gender mixing as abomination, or taboos, which are contrary to religious sensibilities and norms.

Conclusion

As discussed above, according to al-Banna, Fadlallah, and Hizbullah, the concept of *maslaha* legitimises purposeful dancing as a public performance. All three concur that an artistic practice or expression is sanctioned *if and only if* [46] it satisfies two conditions: (1) purposeful, and (2) the advantage (*maslaha*) behind it should outweigh the disadvantage (*mafsadah*). In other words, one ought to weigh the positive and negative consequences before making any decision or resorting to any course of action: simply stated, 'the good should outweigh the bad'. All three view Islam as the 'religion of moderation' that believes in 'justice as fairness' and upholds human worth, value, and dignity. They argued that Islam is social practice and that Islamic law is a socially constructed phenomenon that can account for complexities in modern life, thus solving the apparent problematic of displaying the female body in public space, while catering to Muslim norms and religious sensibilities. We have seen that Hizbullah relates *maslaha* to reform, resistance, mobilisation, and political struggle; for that reason, the party regards art as 'resistance art'.

First, I dealt with the methodology, and then the practice. Although al-Banna's methodology in legitimising his discourses seems different than that of Hizbullah and Fadlallah, it bears a striking resemblance to Shi'ite jurisprudence, thus making the end result for both parties the same: that is, al-Banna, on the one hand, and Hizbullah and Fadlallah, on the other hand: purposefulness, *maslaha*, and *hasanat* justify and legitimise female performance in public space for a mixed audience. Islamic jurisprudential concepts of purposefulness; *maslaha* (interest, advantage) – *mafsadah* (vice, disadvantage) in the Shi'ite tradition; and their counterpart *hasanat* (good deeds) – *sayyi'at* (bad deeds) in the Sunni tradition, legitimise such practices and shoulder them with Islamic credentials. These prove to be a common ground among the erudite Sunni religious scholar Gamal al-Banna – the brother of Hasan al-Banna, the founder of the Muslim Brotherhood in Egypt; the late Ayatullah Fadlallah – the highest ranking Lebanese religious authority who is known for his progressive views, especially when it pertains to women, and the Lebanese resistance movement Hizbullah that seems to put Fadlallah's discourses into practice. By fully exercising its agency, Hizbullah views cultural politics, especially performance in public space, as conducive to empowerment (*tamkin*), in the Qur'anic sense of the term. This article endeavoured to demonstrate that the Lebanese Islamic movement Hizbullah, not only seems to be an embodiment of Fadlallah's and al-Banna's views on the permissibility of a female to perform in public space, but more importantly, a practical illustration that puts the religious scholars' discourses into practice. On the one hand, there appears to be a general confusion in al-Banna's piece between 'actor' and 'activity', that is, 'dancer' who can be a good person, and the activity, 'dance', which remains bad; on the other hand, the Lebanese case is about the activity of female dancing becoming purposeful under certain circumstances.

Building on the aforementioned, this article discussed the concept of purposeful art or 'resistance art' of Hizbullah and the attempt in Egypt by Gamal al-Banna to include dance into the concept of purposeful art. I have argued that the jurisprudential concepts of *maslaha* and *hasanat* legitimise dancing as a purposeful (*hadif*) public performance. I have demonstrated that Hizbullah regards performance as both a 'resistance public' (i.e. as a counter cultural identity against the hegemony and lack of legitimacy of the state and its institutions) and as a counter-public to other Islamic movements who consider acting and dancing on stage as well as gender mixing as abominations, or taboos, which are contrary to religious sensibilities and norms. On the contrary, Hizbullah's resistance art sanctions mixing of the sexes within the domain of religious safeguards, which cater to the religious sensibilities of the mixed audience and uphold the values of the Islamic cultural sphere. I think that of all cultural expressions in Muslim contexts displaying the female body in a gender mixed public space seem to be the most problematic (Tabboni 2006; Geulen: 2006; Göle 2006; Van Nieuwkerk 2003, 1998, and

1995). In spite of that, al-Banna, Fadlallah, and Hizbullah illustrate that such problematic could be overcome through the concerted effort of conferring a novel reading of the sources in line with the progressive shifts that modern society is undergoing.

References

Abbas, F. (2009). *Zaman Al-Intasarat [Days of Victory]*. Beirut: Dar Al-Hadi.

Alagha, J. (2011). 'Pious Entertainment: Hizbullah's Islamic Cultural Sphere', in Karin. van Nieuwkerk (ed.) *Muslim Rap, Halal Soaps and Revolutionary Theater: Artistic Developments in the Muslim World.* Austin: University of Texas Press, pp. 149-175.

---- (2009). 'A Tug of War: Hizbullah, Participation, and Contestation in the Lebanese Public Sphere'. In S. Shami (ed.) *Publics, Politics and Participation: Locating the Public Sphere in the Middle East and North Africa.* New York: Social Science Research Council of America, pp. 457-487.

---- (2006). *The Shifts in Hizbullah's Ideology*, Amsterdam: Amsterdam University Press.

Ali, A. Y. (1993). *The Holy Qur'an: Translation and Commentary*, Fourth printing. Lahore: Islamic Propagation Centre.

Calhoun, C. (2003). 'The Democratic Integration of Europe: Interests, Identity, and the Public Sphere', in M. Berezin and M. Schain (eds.), *Europe without Borders: Re-Mapping Territory, Citizenship and Identity in a Transnational Age*. Baltimore: Johns Hopkins University Press, pp. 243-274.

Fadlallah, M. H. (2009) *Al-Ijtihad Byna Asr Al-Madi wa Afaq Al-Mustaqbal* [Jurisprudence Between the Shackles of the Past and the Horizons of the Future]. Beirut: Al-Markaz al-Thaqafi al-'Arabi.

Fraser, N. (1992). 'Rethinking the public sphere: a contribution to the critique of actually existing democracy'. In C. Calhoun (ed.), *Habermas and the Public Sphere*. Cambridge: MIT Press, pp. 109-142.

Geulen, C. (2006). 'Reflection on the History and Theory of the Public', In N. Göle and L. Ammann (eds.) *Islam in Public: Turkey, Iran, and Europe*. Istanbul: Istanbul Bilgi University Press, pp. 45-76.

Giddens, A. (1990). *Consequences of Modernity*. Cambridge: Polity Press.

Göle, N. and L. Ammann (eds.) (2006). *Islam in Public: Turkey, Iran, and Europe*. Istanbul: Istanbul Bilgi University Press.

Hafez, K. (2010). *Radicalism and Political Reform in the Islamic and Western Worlds*. Cambridge: Cambridge University Press.

LeVine, M. and A. Salvatore. 'Religious Mobilization and the Public Sphere: Reflections on Alternative Genealogies', in Seteney Shami (ed.) *Publics, Politics and Participation: Locating the Public Sphere in the Middle East and North Africa*. New York: Social Science Research Council of America, pp. 65-90.

Roy, O. (1994). *The Failure of Political Islam*. Cambridge: Harvard University Press.

Shami, S. (ed.) (2009). *Publics, Politics and Participation: Locating the Public Sphere in the Middle*

East and North Africa. New York: Social Science Research Council of America.
Tabboni, S. (2006). "Differences in Public Space," in N. Göle and L. Ammann (eds.) *Islam in Public: Turkey, Iran, and Europe*. Istanbul: Istanbul Bilgi University Press, pp. 461-479.
Van Nieuwkerk, K. (2011). 'Of Morals, Missions and the Market New Religiosity and "Art with a Mission" in Egypt', in K. van Nieuwkerk (ed.) *Muslim Rap, Halal Soaps and Revolutionary Theater: Artistic Developments in the Muslim World*. Austin: University of Texas Press, pp. 177-204.
---- (2003). 'On religion, gender, and performing: female performers and repentance in Egypt', in T. Magrini (ed.), *Music and Gender: Perspectives from the Mediterranean*, Chicago: The University of Chicago Press, pp. 267-286.
---- (1998). 'Changing images and shifting identities: female performers in Egypt', in S. Zuhur (ed.), *Images of Enchantment: Visual and Performing Arts of the Middle East*, Cairo: the American University in Cairo Press, pp. 21-35.
---- (1995). *A Trade Like Any Other: Female Singers and Dancers in Egypt*. Austin: University of Texas Press.
Warner, M. (2002). *Publics and Counterpublics*. New York: Zone Books.

Notes

1. In broad letters occupying the last page of the July 23, 2009 issue.
2. In its 1893 issue, on page 20.
3. http://www.almasry-alyoum.com/article2.aspx?ArticleID=222982 (accessed August 19, 2009), including the 66 comments.
4. http://weekly.ahram.org.eg/1999/450/cu4.htm (Accessed on November 08, 2009).
5. We will see later that this is in conformity with al-Banna's employment of the Qur'anic dictum (101: 6-9): 'Good deeds outweigh the bad'.
6. http://weekly.ahram.org.eg/1999/450/cu4.htm (Accessed on November 08, 2009).
7. http://www.almasry-alyoum.com/article2.aspx?ArticleID=222982 (accessed on August 19, 2009).
8. See al-Banna's article: 'Islam is Appropriate for Every Place and Time', (accessed on April 26, 2008) http://www.metransparent.com/spip.php?page=article&id_article=3756&var_lang=ar&lang=ar
9. It seems that al-Banna is indirectly targeting the Salafis. In another podium, he argued that Salafi thinking 'freezes' Islam and 'radicalises' Islamic thought rendering it 'intransigent, reactionary, and backward-looking'. Al-Banna made this statement when al-Azhar, the most important religious establishment in Egypt, confiscated his book entitled *The Muslim Woman between Liberating the Qur'an and the Rigidity of Religious Scholars*, likening al-Azhar's behaviour to the Catholic's Church inquisition courts in the Middle Ages. In that book al-Banna argued, "There is no religious necessity for a woman to wear the veil." In other words, he considered that 'Veiling is not a religious duty'. This reasoning ties in nicely with Fadlallah's argument of 'placing a veil on her heart and desires', if societal conditions prevent her from wearing an actual veil. http://www.metransparent.com/spip.php?page=article&id_article=4027&var_lang=ar&lang=at (Accessed on June 16, 2008).
10. http://www.almasry-alyoum.com/article2.aspx?ArticleID=222982 (accessed on August 19, 2009).
11. Kai Hafez blasts the 'liberal' Egyptian scholar Abu Zayd as a 'deconstructivist' who is 'imparting an approach to the holy texts rather than conceiving a new doctrine' (2010: 38).
12. 'Dancing and Islam, can they be in harmony?', *Al-Masry Al-Youm* 1893 (August 19, 2009), p. 20.
13. Qur'an (7:33): 'The things that my Lord has indeed forbidden are: shameful deeds/debaucheries, whether open or secret'.
14. 'Dancing and Islam, can they be in harmony?', *Al-Masry Al-Youm* 1893 (August 19, 2009), p. 20.
15. Prohibited and sanctioned jobs: http://arabic.bayynat.org.lb/mbayynat/books/fatawa/j2m1b3f1m1.htm (Accessed on July10, 2010)
16. The Jurisprudence of Art, http://english.bayynat.org.lb/se_002/jurisprudence/art.htm (accessed on July 17, 2009).
17. Ibid. Concerning cultural modernity, Habermas has argued that a secular society 'is

not completely without religion, but religion loses its coercive character through the process of secularization' (Hafez 2010: 30).

18. Prohibited and sanctioned jobs: http://arabic.bayynat.org.lb/mbayynat/books/fatawa/j2m1b3f1m1.htm (Accessed on July 10, 2010)
19. Prohibited and sanctioned jobs: http://arabic.bayynat.org.lb/mbayynat/books/fatawa/j2m1b3f1m1.htm (Accessed on July 10, 2010)
20. http://arabic.bayynat.org.lb/mbayynat/books/nadwas/fikr195q5.htm (Accessed on July 10, 2010)
21. Prohibited and sanctioned jobs: http://arabic.bayynat.org.lb/mbayynat/books/fatawa/j2m1b3f1m1.htm (Accessed on July 10, 2010).
22. The Jurisprudence of Art: http://english.bayynat.org.lb/se_002/jurisprudence/art.htm (Accessed on July 10, 2010).
23. Personal interview, August 04, 2009.
24. Ibid.
25. http://www.almasry-alyoum.com/article2.aspx?ArticleID=222982 (accessed on August 19, 2009).
26. Ibid.
27. Hizbullah's Shaykh Akram Barakat argues along similar lines (see below).
28. In reference to the many Qur'anic verses that uphold such a concept, for instance (22:41).
29. http://english.bayynat.org.lb/se_002/islamicinsights/elaph_p2.htm:'Ruling on Songs by M.H. Fadlallah part (2)' (accessed on July 17, 2009).
30. See the section entitled, 'Imposing Injunctions between *Masalih* and *Mafasid*' (*fard al-ahkam bayna al-masalih was al-mafasid*).
31. He regarded the restitution of virginity as any plastic surgery that any woman is entitled to, especially if the loss of virginity resulted from an accident or rape. However, the operation is absolutely *haraam* if it is intended to deceive the husband and defile the institution of marriage. See the interview with Fadlallah's representative Shaykh Husayn Abdallah in the programme entitled 'For Publication' (*lel-Nasher*) presented by Tony Khalife, NTV Lebanon, June 26, 2010.http://www.aljadeed.tv/newtvsat/Programs/General/Global/Default.aspx?pr_id=459
32. Personal interview, August 04, 2009.
33. That is to say, common to both Sunnis and Shi'ites.
34. http://www.almasry-alyoum.com/article2.aspx?ArticleID=222982 (accessed on August 19, 2009).
35. Personal interview, October 16, 2009.
36. See Qasim's introduction to ('Abbas 2009: 6-7). The book contains a host of mobilisational poems, including the most played song after the July 2006 war: '*Nasrak Hazz al-Dini* (Your Victory Shook the World)': http://www.welaya-hlb.com/palysong.php?id=84; http://www.welaya-hlb.com/sub.php?op=new#. (Accessed on September 26, 2009). This book has been published to commemorate 'Beirut as an International Book Capital'. Poet Fadi 'Abbas is the minutes taker (*amin al-sirr*) of *Al-Ma'arif Al-Hikmiyya* College.

37. Personal interview, October 22, 2009.
38. Personal interview, August 10, 2009.
39. Personal interview, February 15, 2010.
40. Interviews conducted in 2009 with Shaykh Akram Barakat, Skaykh 'Ali Daher, and Shaykh Shafiq Jaradi.
41. Interview with Shaykh Muhammad Kawtharani, Political Council member and the responsible for the Iraqi file (a close aide to Sayyid Hasan Nasrallah), January 20, 2010.
42. Personal interview, October 21, 2009.
43. Personal interview, August 04, 2009.
44. Personal interview, October 06, 2009.
45. Personal Interview, August 04, 2009.
46. 'If and only if' is a mathematical formulation, which implies that it is a must that both conditions should be satisfied.